Everything You Need to Know About

BEING
HIV-POSITIVE

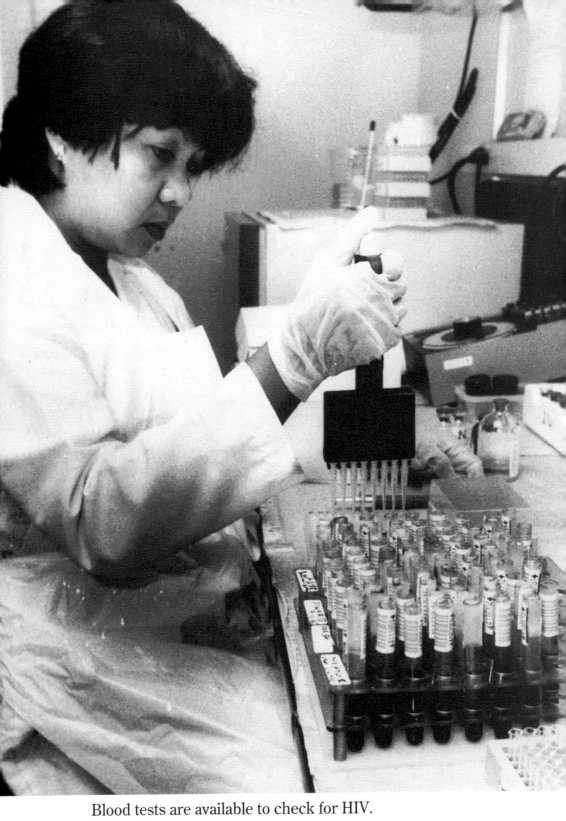

Blood tests are available to check for HIV.

Everything You Need to Know About

BEING HIV-POSITIVE

Amy Shire

THE ROSEN PUBLISHING GROUP, INC.
NEW YORK

Special thanks to Brenda Garza at the Centers for Disease Control and Prevention (CDC) for ensuring the accuracy of the technical sections of this book.

To my parents and Harold and Lindy

Acknowledgments

I would like to thank my colleagues in the Division of AIDS Services Planning Unit for their help and support. Whether or not they were specifically aware of the writing of this book, their compassion, commitment to their work, and to one another, extraordinary sense of teamwork, and wicked sense of humor have been a tremendous source of sustenance and pleasure to me.

I would also like to thank Sara and Hillary for their invaluable suggestions and limitless lending libraries; and especially the teenagers and staff of the Montefiore Adolescent Program, without whom this book could not have been completed. I hope it speaks the truth to you, as you have so generously been able to do with me.

Published in 1994, 1998 by The Rosen Publishing Group, Inc.
29 East 21st Street, New York, New York 10010

Copyright © 1994, 1998 by The Rosen Publishing Group, Inc.

Revised Edition 1998

Library of Congress Cataloging-in-Publication Data

Shire, Amy.
    Everything you need to know about being HIV positive / Amy Shire.
        p.   cm. (The Need to Know Library)
    Includes bibliographical references and index.
    ISBN 0-8239-2614-1
    1. HIV infections—Juvenile literature. [1. HIV (Viruses). 2. AIDS (Disease).]
I. Title. II. Series.
RC607.A26S493 1994
362.1'869792—dc20   94-13502
                                                                              CIP
                                                                              AC

Manufactured in the United States of America

Contents

Feelings of loneliness and isolation may come with the knowledge of being HIV-positive.

Chapter 1

The Different Faces of HIV

*E*velyn is frightened. She thinks that she may have HIV, the virus that causes AIDS. She has some of the symptoms of HIV infection: she's lost a lot of weight recently, she's always tired, and she has sores in her mouth. Evelyn has heard about HIV, but she never thought it would happen to her. She thinks she got HIV by sharing heroin needles with her boyfriend Hal and a few of their friends. Someone's HIV-infected blood must have gotten into her body when she was shooting up.

"What am I going to do? What am I going to tell my parents?" Evelyn wondered. "Since I've been dating Hal, they think I've been doing drugs. I kept denying it, but now I am going to have to tell them. I feel ashamed and scared."

Dan has hemophilia. It is a hereditary disease that prevents his blood from clotting. When he was little he had a blood transfusion. That was before blood and blood products were tested for HIV antibodies. Dan became infected with the virus.

HIV was in Dan's body for ten years before he had any symptoms. Now Dan is getting sick. He is upset because he has HIV even though he didn't do anything that he shouldn't have. He didn't have unprotected sex, he didn't use drugs.

"Most days I get really angry. Why did this have to happen to me? It's so unfair!"

Tanya was only seventeen when she had a baby. She was HIV-positive when her daughter, Noelle, was born just a year ago. Tanya got the virus from Noelle's father who was an injection drug user. Luckily, Tanya didn't pass the virus on to Noelle.

Tanya has started going to an AIDS day program where she receives counseling and has learned computer skills so she can get a job.

What Tanya has learned at the day program helps her deal with her problems.

"It's been rough, but for my daughter's sake I keep going. Now my biggest worry is finding somebody to take care of Noelle if I die."

About a year ago, Greg was really sick. He was HIV-positive and his body wasn't responding to AZT, an antiviral drug used to slow down HIV.

"I was pretty worried. The drugs weren't working as well as my doctor and I had hoped. But then he started me on the new combination drugs."

Now Greg has an undetectable level of the virus in his body. He still has the virus, but he has taken control of his health again.

"When I was in high school I was on the track team," Greg says. *"I was pretty good, too. I didn't think I'd ever compete again because of how weak I was. But after a year of the combination therapy, I feel great. I am going to compete in a triathlon next week!"*

Their stories are all different and although they may not realize it yet, these four teens have one thing in common: hope. Hope that with new drug therapies and new breakthroughs in research they will live healthier, longer lives. Perhaps long enough to see a cure for AIDS.

HOW HIV (THE AIDS VIRUS) AFFECTS THE IMMUNE SYSTEM

Normal Immune System

A person with a healthy immune system has various types of lymphocytes that combat any invading disease organisms.

Immune System in an AIDS Victim

A person with the HIV virus has a weakened immune system. In some cases, this weakness may lead to the series of infections known as AIDS.

Disease organisms   **T4-lymphocytes**

HIV   **T4- lymphocytes**

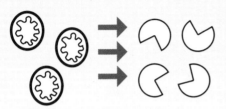

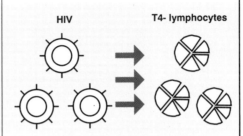

1 T4-lymphocytes and other immune system components in the body are alerted when they detect disease organisms.

1 HIV (the AIDS virus) actually multiplies within the body's T4 -lymphocytes and may ultimately destroy them.

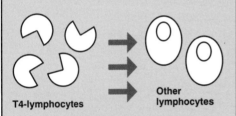

T4-lymphocytes   **Other lymphocytes**

Destroyed T4-lymphocytes

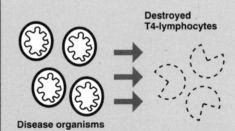

Disease organisms

2 In response to the invading organisms, the T4-lymphocytes help to regulate the response of other lymphocytes (cells of the immune system)

2 When the disease organisms invade other areas of the body, the immune responses may fail, due to absence of the vital T4-lymphocytes.

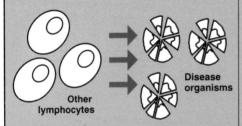

Other lymphocytes   **Disease organisms**

Disease organisms

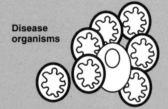

3 The alerted lymphocytes then attack and destroy the disease organisms in various ways.

3 The disease organisms may overwhelm the immune system and lead to a series of infections known commonly as AIDS.

Chapter 2

Being HIV-Positive

L et's begin with a few definitions. HIV is short for human immunodeficiency virus. A virus is a small organism (living thing)—too small to see without a microscope—that can exist inside people's cells and make them sick. Human, of course, makes it clear that this virus lives in people. Immunodeficiency refers to the body's immune system, the cells that fight infection. Someone who is immunodeficient does not have enough of the kinds of cells needed to protect the body from infections and diseases.

How Do I Know I Have HIV?

People find out they have HIV by getting tested. One test (called an ELISA test) is a blood test. It does not detect the actual presence of HIV; it measures the amount of immune cells—called antibodies—that try to combat HIV. Testing "positive" for HIV means that HIV antibodies showed up in the results, and that the virus is in your body. HIV can be in your body for three to six months before the antibodies show up on an HIV test. If you test negative, you should be tested again three to six months after exposure to be sure.

Everyone who is tested for HIV should have counseling. People whose results are positive will need time to absorb the information and to begin planning what they will do next.

When Marisa found out she was HIV-positive, she was stunned. All she could think about was what she should do about taking care of her little girl. Her doctor let her think through her thoughts for a while. He wanted her to do whatever she felt like doing or saying at that moment. The doctor let Marisa know that she wasn't dying, and that there were many things she could do right away that would help her live longer and enjoy her life.

Does Having HIV Mean I Have AIDS?

AIDS stands for acquired immunodeficiency syndrome. Acquired means something you got after you were born. Immunodeficiency means your immune system lacks what it needs to protect you against illness. Syndrome is a pattern of signs or symptoms of illness that occur over a period of time.

Some people think that being HIV-positive is the same as having AIDS. It's not. Having HIV means you have the virus in your body. However, you can feel perfectly fine and healthy for a very long time. Some people have lived as long as fifteen years or more without being sick. This stage is called being asymptomatic, which means having no symptoms.

Having AIDS, on the other hand, means you are sick with one or more illnesses. HIV has weakened your immune system and made you susceptible to these illnesses. People with AIDS develop serious illnesses, may get better, and then may get sick again in a recurring cycle. Eventually, most people with AIDS die from one of these illnesses.

What It's Like to Have AIDS

Probably one of the scariest things about AIDS is that it is hard to predict what kind of illness will hit you and when. People with AIDS can get rare diseases, such as Kaposi's sarcoma (a form of cancer) and other opportunistic infections—infections that don't usually show up in people whose immune systems are healthy. Some of these infections are TB (tuberculosis) and a type of pneumonia called PCP (*Pneumocystis carinii*). Women can get the same infections as men and are at greater risk of getting cervical cancer.

At present, there is no vaccine for HIV or a cure for AIDS. But several kinds of drugs are used to slow down the effects of the disease.

How You Can—and Cannot—Get HIV

If you are HIV-positive, you may already know or be able to guess how you got it. HIV is transmitted through contact with infected semen (the fluid that comes from the penis when a man has an orgasm, or "comes"), vaginal fluids, or blood, or it is passed from mother to child during pregnancy or childbirth. There is also some evidence that HIV can be transmitted from mother to child through breast milk. Before 1985, it was possible to get HIV through blood transfusions and the plasma used by hemophiliacs (people with a blood disease)

You cannot get HIV through casual social contact, such as sharing meals.

because there was not yet a way to test the blood supply for HIV. Now all donated blood is carefully tested, and the blood supply in the United States and Europe is very safe.

You *cannot* get or pass on HIV by touching someone, hugging, dry kissing, eating from someone else's plate or having someone eat off of your plate, mosquito bites, toilet seats, pools, playing sports, shaking hands, sneezing... Do you get the picture? Most casual activities are perfectly safe to do with people with HIV or AIDS. If you have a question about a particular activity, there are phone numbers listed in the back of this book that you can call to ask any question. Or you may prefer to ask your doctor or nurse. Don't be afraid to ask; there is no such thing as a silly question, especially when it comes to HIV and AIDS.

How to Prevent HIV from Spreading

If you are HIV-positive, it is very important that you learn how to prevent the virus from spreading. This is true for two reasons: protecting others *and* protecting yourself. You may ask, "Well, since I'm already infected, why should it matter to me?" The answer is that you can become *re-infected* by someone else who is HIV-positive, which may weaken your immune system further and be harmful to you. So, for your own best interest, and to safeguard others, avoid the transmission of HIV at all costs.

To prevent HIV from spreading you must be careful not to exchange the body fluids that may contain the virus. These fluids include mainly blood, semen, vaginal secretions, and menstrual blood. Exposure to these body fluids happens most often through sex or injection drug use. HIV is not passed through saliva, tears, sweat, urine, or feces.

Abstinence

Practicing safer sex is wise, but not having sex protects best. Whatever the uncertainties about transmitting or contracting HIV, one thing is certain: if you're not having sex, you cannot transmit or get HIV. Not having sex at all is called abstinence.

For those who are sexually active, deciding whether or not to be abstinent requires taking a long, hard look at your life. What role does sex play in your life? Is it worth the risk of becoming infected with HIV or any other sexually transmitted disease?

If you're not sexually active yet, you can't transmit or get HIV. That's a very good reason to wait before starting to have sex. If you choose to say no to sex, that's okay, even if your friends are sexually active. The best time to become sexually active is when you decide it is. When you decide that you're ready, hopefully it will be with someone you care about. If you and your partner care about each other, then you'll be smart enough to take precautions to avoid unwanted pregnancy and sexually transmitted diseases and HIV.

Couples must take responsibility to prevent spreading HIV.

Safer Sex

If you decide to have sex, have safer sex. Use a new latex condom every time you have sex. This will help prevent someone else's bodily fluids from getting inside your body, possibly infecting you with HIV. Never let your semen or blood get into someone else's body.

Use only latex condoms and water-based lubricants for vaginal or anal intercourse. This is the only way to make intercourse safer.

Even oral sex has risks. HIV can pass through the cells in your mouth and spread throughout your body. Plus, cuts and sores inside your mouth are common. If you are having oral sex, HIV-infected semen or vaginal fluids can get into those cuts and sores and infect you.

Kissing is safe, but don't deep kiss if there are open sores or cuts in your mouth or right after flossing and brushing. Take these precautions to prevent the exchange of blood.

Condoms

A condom is a protective barrier that is worn on the penis during sexual intercourse. Condoms help prevent pregnancy and HIV infection by stopping HIV-carrying semen before it can enter another person's body. You should only use latex condoms. Condoms made from other material, such as lambskin, are not as strong. There are female condoms available as well.

Here is how to use a condom correctly:

Roll the condom all the way down the shaft of the erect penis to its base. Leave room at the tip for the semen to collect.

If you choose to use a lubricant, only use a water-based lubricant such as K-Y Jelly. Oil-based lubricants such as Vaseline can weaken the latex and cause the condom to leak or break. After ejaculation, pull out gently while the penis is still erect. Take the condom off carefully so the semen doesn't spill. Condoms can be used only once.

The female condom is a plastic sheath that a woman can insert into her vagina to prevent contact of sexual fluids. It should not be used at the same time as a male condom.

Drug Use

If you are injecting drugs of any kind—**stop**. This advice is for your general health and well-being and to prevent HIV transmission. Talk to an adult whom you trust and get yourself into treatment. If you continue to inject drugs, at least do it more safely: don't share needles and use a clean, sterile needle each time. If sterile neeedles are not available, then clean your works (needles and syringes) with bleach for at least thirty seconds before each use. Blood left on the needle or in the syringe can be transferred from one person to another.

Think about HIV and other drugs, too, such as marijuana and alcohol. Even if you are not injecting, drugs can impair your judgment. If you are in sexual situations and using drugs or alcohol, you may be less likely to think about safer sex.

A positive diagnosis of HIV can cause emotional distress. The comfort of friends will be helpful.

Chapter 3

You're HIV-Positive.
Now What?

W hen you are first diagnosed with HIV, many feelings may come to the surface: fear, anger, sadness, disbelief, rebelliousness, confusion. These and other feelings are all natural reactions to news that is shocking and upsetting.

People think there must be some mistake. Or they feel numb because the news is too much to absorb all at once. These are signs of denial, or letting yourself pretend that things aren't the way they really are. "This can't happen to me! I'm different." Have you said that to yourself? If so, you are not alone; many people have that reaction when they are diagnosed with HIV. You are probably scared, and everyone wants to push away things they are scared of. Also, taking this attitude can calm you a little in the short run; you feel less stress if you think there is nothing to worry about. Marco felt that way a lot when he was on the street. He'd say to himself, "I'll be off the street as soon as I find an acting job." That enabled him to feel better about himself, but it did nothing to get him out of danger. In the long run, being in denial can harm you. You will be less likely to take care of yourself and others if you continue to pretend you are not infected with HIV.

Denial comes from fear. Everyone fears the unknown, pain, and dying. For some people it can be overwhelming. One way to overcome fear is knowledge. Learning as much as you can about HIV will take away some of the anxiety.

Another way to combat fear is to take things one step at a time. If you look at all aspects of your future at once, it can be too much to deal with. Break it down a little. Set yourself some goals for the next week, the next month, the next several months. Getting panicky over the distant future will only make you miserable. You need to face the reality of having HIV without letting it take over, so you can continue living your life.

When Claudia found out she was HIV-positive, she was about to have some braces put on her teeth. However, in the days after her test, feeling hopeless and unhappy, she thought: "Why should I bother fixing my teeth? I'm just going to die anyway." Gradually, Claudia came to terms with her

Talking to a professional counselor can help you to better understand HIV.

fears and realized that probably she had many
years ahead of her. She decided to take her life
seriously—she remade her appointment to get the
braces put on.

One of the hardest emotions to deal with is
anger. "Why me?" is often people's first question
when they learn they are HIV-positive. "It's not
fair! I've always been a good person. . ." Sometimes the anger is directed toward the rest of the
world that is not infected, or toward the person
who possibly has been the route of infection.
People feel bitter, and sometimes revengeful.

Sometimes, the anger is directed inward, and
the person becomes very depressed. Claudia re-
membered: "When I found out I had HIV, I wanted
to stay away from everyone who loved me. . ."
Often, people blame themselves for their illness: If
only they hadn't had sex, or weren't gay, or didn't
hang around with people who did drugs, they
wouldn't be in this situation. They think having
HIV must be a punishment. Sometimes they don't
even realize they feel this way.

Gracia, for example, became addicted to crack
at the age of 14. Because she had no other income,
she had sex with the crack dealers to pay for her
drugs. Soon she was feeling very bad about herself
and wanted to stop, but she was controlled by her
addiction. After a while, she met a health outreach
worker who persuaded her to come to a mobile
clinic for care. She tested positive for HIV.

Nothing seemed to matter to Gracia after that. She became depressed, and continued to have unprotected sex because she was so angry with herself and the rest of the world. Finally, Gracia found a support group run by a local hospital, where she learned a less harsh way of looking at herself. Now she calls what she was doing "slow suicide."

Many people are afraid of feeling angry. Anger is such a powerful emotion. But it is important to admit to yourself that you are angry, if that's what you are feeling. Having HIV *is* unfair. Dan, the teen with hemophilia that we met in chapter one, often felt this way. He needed blood products before scientists new how to test blood for HIV antibodies. He felt that he had been cheated out of a chance to use an uninfected blood supply.

Getting HIV isn't always entirely due to bad luck, although in Dan's case it was. Doing certain things, such as having unprotected sex or sharing needles, greatly increases your chances of getting HIV.

But what if you do practice safer sex and the condom breaks, or slips off? You took the right precautions but contracted HIV anyway. It is unfair. You do have a right to be angry.

People with HIV say that what has been most helpful to them is the ability to move beyond their anger. Learning to accept that they are HIV-positive has enabled them to get past feeling bitter and to refocus their lives.

People who know the facts about HIV are less likely to be judgmental.

Chapter 4

How Will People See Me?

Many people worry about how others will react to the fact that they have HIV. When Alejandro first found out he was HIV-positive, he felt ashamed and afraid that others would look down on him. "What will my family and friends think of me? Will they reject me? Do I have to tell people that I'm gay as well as that I have HIV?"

Sad to say, there is some reason for Alejandro to be concerned. People who don't know better *stigmatize* people with HIV or AIDS. They think negative things about them without having any valid reason to do so.

Some people are judgmental. They are only concerned about *how* someone gets the virus, and then they judge the person's behavior. They label people who are HIV-positive as "innocent" or "guilty," "good" or "bad." For example, children are often seen as innocent victims, whereas adults—including young adults—are seen as having "done something" to bring HIV on themselves.

The most important thing is not to adopt other people's negative judgments about you. HIV is a virus, not a sign of having behaved badly. No one gets HIV on purpose.

The picture has gotten somewhat brighter, though. Despite widespread ignorance and prejudice, there is more general awareness about HIV and AIDS today. And with better understanding of the disease, people tend to be more sympathetic.

You will find people who will act with compassion and sympathy and show that they love and accept you. Sometimes it may be the ones you least expect—schoolmates, coworkers, neighbors. Seek these people out. They are the ones of true value. They will help sustain you as much or more than any medication.

Chapter 5

Your Legal Rights

When you have HIV or AIDS, you have certain legal rights: the right to keep your status private (confidentiality), the right to agree to HIV testing and treatment (informed consent), and the right to receive good medical care. Because the exact legal rights vary from state to state, for specific information it's best to call the Department of Public Health or an AIDS hot line in your area. This chapter outlines some of the important facts you need to know.

Confidentiality

Because HIV is such a personal matter, and because of the stigma surrounding the disease, confidentiality is extremely important for people with HIV and AIDS.

How private you can be about HIV begins with how and where you are tested. When you were tested for HIV, you were tested either anonymously or confidentially. If you were tested at an *anonymous* testing site, no one knows you by name, and the results were not written down; only a number went on your lab slip. If you were tested *confidentially*, such as in a doctor's office or clinic, your doctor and possibly other health professionals or staff know your HIV status. They are not supposed to reveal information outside the office without your permission, but they can use the information to begin the proper treatment for you. Generally, most social service and health institutions consider it all right to share information within their organization without getting your permission directly. To talk to a particular person or agency on the outside, they need to ask you first. Then you usually need to sign a release form of some kind.

You may want to ask the health or social service agency working with you about your medical records. You should know if HIV information is included in your records and who has access to your records.

Partner Notification

Partner notification refers to telling sexual or drug partners of HIV-positive people that they have been exposed to the virus. Laws about sharing this particular information differ among the states.

Sexual partners need to be honest with each other about their past sexual activities.

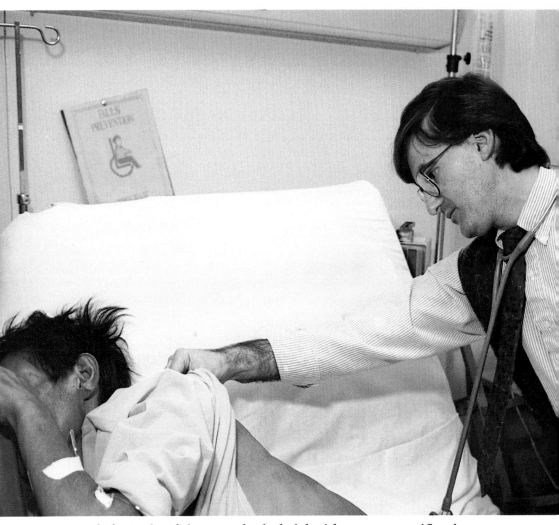

A doctor's advice may be helpful with partner notification.

In New York State, for example, partner notification
rules are the same for teenagers as for adults. Your
physician may ask you for the names of people with
whom you have had sex or shared needles. He or
she will encourage you to tell those persons that
you have been tested and are HIV-positive. If you
are unwilling to do that, your doctor can notify

them that they have been exposed to HIV. Your
doctor cannot reveal your name to the people whom
you have exposed to the virus or tell them how they
have been exposed. The only people who are
allowed to contact your partners are your doctor or
a person you choose to do this for you. Laws about
partner notification are different in each state.

Consent

Most adolescents under the age of eighteen are
considered minors. They do not have the same legal
rights as adults. Minors are not allowed to make
certain decisions for themselves, such as signing a
contract or receiving certain kinds of medical care.
However, teenagers may make their own decisions
in some areas of health care dealing with HIV.

States have different laws and regulations
concerning such decisions. For instance, in New York
any teenager who understands the purpose of the HIV
test may be tested without an adult's permission.

As a teen your HIV status cannot be revealed
without your permission, with some exceptions.
For instance, parents or guardians may be told
your HIV status if it becomes medically necessary
to do so.

Also, prison officials, the military, and foster care
and adoption agencies can request information
about your HIV status. HIV status may also be
released in cases of sexual assault or child abuse.

Written consent to reveal HIV-related

information is not necessary for health-care providers working in the same institution; however it is required for any outside agency or facility trying to gain access to your records.

You should seriously consider telling your parents or guardian your HIV status. They can provide the financial and emotional support you need at this time. However, some teens don't feel comfortable confiding in adults.

For teenagers who are on their own, or who have children of their own, some states have categories called "mature" or "emancipated" minors. There are no hard and fast rules as to who qualifies. Generally, the terms refer to people under the age of eighteen who have a child, live on their own and support themselves, or have been abandoned by their parents or guardians. They are legally able to make certain decisions for themselves. You need legal and social service assistance to become an "emancipated minor."

As you can see, the rules for consent are complex and detailed. Some questions to keep in mind about treatment are the following:

- What does a "release of information" do in your state?
- What services are medical and social service providers permitted to give you without the consent of a parent or guardian?
- For what kinds of treatment do you need a parent's or guardian's permission?

Human Rights

No one can be discriminated against because he or she is HIV-positive or has AIDS. This means you cannot:

- be kicked out of school
- be denied medical treatment
- be fired from a job
- be evicted from an apartment solely on the grounds that you have HIV or AIDS.

Most states have a Commission of Human Rights that oversees these laws and can step in when there are violations.

Everyone who is HIV-positive or has AIDS has the right to good medical treatment. No one can be denied treatment on the grounds of having HIV or AIDS. That is the law everywhere.

Getting rest and eating healthful foods are important to keep the immune system working.

Chapter 6

Taking Care of Yourself

Let's break things down so they don't seem so scary and overwhelming. Think about the parts of you that need to be taken care of: your body, your mind, and your spirit. These parts are connected, but we can talk about them separately.

Your Body
Your Sexual Identity

Taking care of your body is perhaps the first thing you'll think of. For one thing, at this time in your life your body is extremely important to you. Whether or not you have had any sexual experiences, sex is very much on the minds of many young people. So anything that interferes with this can cause frustration and sadness.

If you are HIV-positive and contracted the virus through sex, you may have mixed feelings about sex. It may seem like a dirty or negative thing. If you are experimenting with partners of the same sex, or are defining yourself as gay or lesbian, society sends so many negative messages about this sexual behavior that it can easily make you feel ashamed.

It is very important that you keep a positive self-image, despite any disapproving messages from the outside. Understanding yourself as a sexual person (sometimes called a sexual identity) is a wonderful thing. It's part of your development as a person, of who you are as an individual and how you communicate. Some people say it is a gift of nature, or of God.

However, you are responsible for how you act on your sexual feelings. The choices you make about your sexual behavior will determine whether you or another person are treated well or get hurt. Where HIV is concerned, it is your responsibility to have safer sex if you have sex.

Good Medical Care

When you are HIV-positive, the first step in taking care of yourself is getting good medical care. Find a doctor that you trust who can take care of both your HIV-related and general medical needs. If you don't have a doctor already, ask an HIV counseling clinic for a referral.

While you are HIV-positive but have no symptoms, your doctor will take care of your primary health-care needs, such as treating ordinary colds and flu and giving you regular checkups and, if you are a woman, gynecological care. It's very important that you eat and sleep well. You need a balanced diet with lots of vitamins to keep your immune system healthy, and you need plenty of rest.

It is good to exercise too. You should do something you enjoy, like playing tennis, swimming, or in-line skating. Also, try to stay away from people who are sick. Even if you just get a cold, it will put stress on your immune system that can be harmful to you.

Your doctor will monitor your CD4 (also called T-cell) count. This monitoring is a way of gauging when to start you on certain medicines that will help you keep your immune system functioning.

CD4 cells are the cells in the immune system that are directly harmed by HIV. The more CD4 cells you have, the healthier you stay. Healthy adults may have between 800 and 1,200 CD4 cells in their immune systems. A person with HIV has fewer of these cells. When someone's CD4 cell count has dropped below 200, their immune system is very weak. He or she may be showing symptoms of various AIDS-related diseases and infections. That person is then diagnosed with AIDS.

Some general symptoms of HIV illness include night sweats, fever, extreme tiredness, weakness, and diarrhea, which can lead to loss of appetite and dehydration. Some medications can offset these and other symptoms.

New and Promising HIV Treatments

Good news. According to the U.S. Centers for Disease Control and Prevention (CDC), 1996 marked the first decline in AIDS deaths nationwide since the epidemic began in the early 1980s. From January 1996 through June 1996 the estimated number of AIDS deaths was 13 percent less than the same period in 1995.

The CDC spokesperson said that it was too soon to say what effect new combination drug treatments will have on the downward trend of AIDS deaths. But she did say that protease inhibitors, which are a part of the new treatments, "promise to further lengthen the life spans" of people with AIDS. Still greater reductions in AIDS deaths are expected if the drugs have no serious side effects and if the drugs prove effective for long-term use.

Protease inhibitors work by blocking a component of HIV called protease. Without protease, HIV can't infect new cells. Studies show that when a protease inhibitor is combined with one or more of the established HIV/AIDS medicines, such as AZT, ddI, or 3TC, they work together to attack HIV at different stages of its progression.

This new combination, or "cocktail," therapy has been shown to reduce the level of HIV in the blood-

There are medications available to treat HIV.

stream by up to 99 percent in some patients, including people with long-standing HIV infections. The result: The new treatments could halt or slow the advance of the disease.

Drug research continues. In early 1997 another new class of drugs called non-nucleoside reverse transcriptase inhibitors became available for use in combination therapy. These advances are very promising and new research is being done everyday. Hopefully in the near future a cure will be found.

Clinical Trials

Research into new medications and treatments is ongoing throughout the country. One way to get good medical care and possibly receive new treatments is to enter a *clinical trial*. This is a research experiment involving people who volunteer to test new drugs. They are monitored closely and receive high-quality, free, and regular medical care. A teenager may need a parent's consent to enroll.

Nutrition

It is very important to have a good diet when you are HIV-positive. Eating well will give you the energy you need and help your immune system stay as healthy as possible. Eat from the four major food groups: (1) fish, eggs, beans, and meat; (2) vegetables and fruits (oranges, tomatoes, lettuce, bananas, potatoes); (3) grains and cereals (rice, spaghetti, bread, pancakes, grits, corn); and (4) dairy products (milk, yogurt, cheese). Avoid too much greasy food like potato chips—it gives you only empty calories.

One of the biggest problems people face with HIV infection is weight loss. When you are hungry, *eat*. Don't worry about eating too much, but concentrate on foods that provide nutrition as well as calories. Ice cream, milkshakes, cheesecake, and pizza, for example, have lots of dairy products, which contain protein and vitamins, and lots of calories, all of which are important for you.

People with HIV infection sometimes don't feel like eating. Their medication may make them nauseated, they may have sores in their mouth or diarrhea, or they are tired and just have no appetite. Here are some suggestions that may help with this problem:

- Eat a lot of small meals instead of three large ones; it may relieve the nausea. Eating dry, salty foods like crackers, or bland foods like rice, noodles, eggs, bananas, and bread will also help with nausea.
- Avoid greasy foods, which may give you diarrhea.
- Try using a blender to make your food soft, like baby food. Also, try cold foods like popsicles: They can numb your mouth and ease the pain.

Exercise and Stress Management

One of the best things you can do for yourself is exercise. It is good for your body and will help you to relax. Find something active that you like to do. It could be basketball, gardening, running, walking, swimming, aerobics, yoga, skating, or dancing. If you enjoy it, you're more likely to stick with it.

Having HIV or AIDS can be very stressful. Learning ways to relax can make your body less tense and help you feel more peaceful. How can you do this? Here are some suggestions:

- Find a place where you can be alone and sit quietly. Some people try to empty their minds of all thoughts and meditate.
- Get a massage. This is terrific for relaxing the body and the mind and getting rid of tension.
- Go to the movies.
- Go dancing.
- Do something creative that requires concentration: playing an instrument, painting, or taking photographs.
- Take long walks, by yourself or with someone close to you.

The most important thing to remember in managing stress is not to do too many things at once. Know and respect your limits, and leave plenty of time for yourself.

Your Mind and Spirit

How do you take care of your emotions, your mind and spirit? How can you face the realities of living with HIV? What will it take to convince you that your life is still worthwhile?

Probably the most difficult question people with HIV or AIDS ask is: "Why me? I'm young and just beginning my life. Why might it be cut so short?" Some people find their answers through faith in a higher power. Others find comfort by talking to family and friends. No matter where you turn, though, there is no simple answer to "why?" Try to

People with HIV should try to stay active and enjoy the company of friends.

look past that question and enjoy your life. Take care of yourself and do things that make you happy and make you feel good. You still have control over your attitude toward yourself and your life. If you can maintain a positive attitude, you'll feel better and stronger.

How do you get to that positive attitude? People often go through a process of feeling anger, fear, and depression and eventually learn to accept their situation. Though their condition is always in the back of their minds, they keep busy with the rest of their lives. The road through these difficult emotions has many twists and turns. Some days go easily, others are more troubled.

Counseling and Support Groups

Talking to a counselor or therapist can be extremely helpful in dealing with strong emotions. These are trained professionals who are completely nonjudgmental. They will listen to you and help you understand your emotions. They may also be able to suggest different ways of dealing with your illness and reducing stress.

Sometimes people feel so depressed they think about killing themselves. If this describes you, talk to someone before acting on your feelings. Call any adult you trust. They may be able to help you work your feelings out. Sometimes just talking to someone is all you need. Let him or her help you through this painful time.

Support groups for young people with HIV or AIDS are a great way to make you realize that you are not alone. You can share information and make new friends who know what you are going through and will support you through it. Many people find comfort in such a group, a place where they can be themselves.

Coping with HIV

It takes a lot of internal struggle to cope with HIV and AIDS. You may ask yourself questions most people take years to figure out. What is it that gives my life meaning, and how can I continue to give it meaning now that I have this virus? One thing to realize is that *you are still the same person you were before you were HIV-positive.* How you feel about yourself will affect your attitude toward the illness, as it does toward any other challenge.

The best thing is to continue on the path you've chosen, and change that path as needed. Your life doesn't have to stop having a direction because you are HIV-positive.

It might be instinctive to "speed up" your life. Actually, the opposite is sometimes what's needed: "Slow down and smell the flowers." If you are able to see and appreciate who you are, what you are doing in the present, and what you have in front of you, you can develop a richness in life and be far less trapped than the person who needs to do five things at once to be "living to the fullest."

Talking to a trusted adult can help you sort through the questions.

Chapter 7

Making Decisions

HIV is a disease that makes you grow up faster; there's no way around it. If you are HIV-positive, you are thinking about things and making decisions that other people your age generally don't have to do at all or in the same way.

Disclosure

One of the first questions you will ask yourself if you are HIV-positive is: Whom do I tell? You may want to tell the people you feel closest to, who can best help and support you. You should not feel any pressure to tell anyone. However, to be helped best, both medically and emotionally, will require you to tell some people about your status. This especially includes your parents or guardians and

your doctor. Talk to an adult you trust, whether it's
your parents or a counselor, to help you sort
through these questions.

Telling others is not always easy. "It's always a
risk," many have said. You risk rejection, fear,
harassment, and stigma.

You have to trust your instincts about the particular person. M&M does a lot of probing of
people before he tells them. He mentions visiting
someone in the hospital with HIV, for example, and
watches for clues in the reaction of the person he's
talking to. Phara sometimes feels like bursting out
with it. Yet she doesn't want people to reject her or
to feel sorry for her. Sometimes she makes things
up to protect herself. She will say she's going to
work when she's going to the clinic, for example.
Claudia says, "If someone finds out I'm positive, I
can deal with that. I just don't want to tell them."

If you are sexually active, what about disclosing
to people you think about having sex with? You
need to consider several things: your feelings
about your HIV and that person, your rights, and
your responsibilities. Your *legal right* is to keep
your HIV status private. Your responsibility to that
person, however, involves *ethics*—what is *morally
right* to do. Your feelings may be very complicated
and in conflict with one another.

Here are some questions you may want to ask
yourself: Do I trust this person enough to tell?
What will happen if I tell? How will I feel if this

person doesn't want to have sex with me then? How will I feel about myself if I don't tell? How would I feel if I were the other person? Do I want to have sex with someone whom I don't trust enough to tell?

You may ask yourself: "As long as we're having safer sex, why does anyone need to know?" Because there is no *absolutely* safe sex, an element of risk remains. That's where the "gray area" of right and wrong lies. You need to ask yourself whether you and your partner are equal players if you know something your partner doesn't.

Enjoying Yourself and Taking Care of Others

Having HIV doesn't mean your life stops. You can and should continue to have friends, go out, and socialize. But partying a lot isn't good for you if you don't get enough rest, or if you are taking medications. You may need to moderate your behavior to take care of your health.

You can still date, but again you have choices to make. You can choose not to have sex; it is the safest way not to reinfect yourself or infect someone else. However, if you decide to have sex, the key thing to remember is to have safer sex: Use a condom every time you have sex.

This rule seems simple, but a lot of people have a hard time following it. Some people say that the condom cuts down on the feeling, and that stopping to put it on interrupts the "natural flow" of sex. Brian doesn't like having to pull out so soon after sex. "Lingering is part of feeling close, keeping the moment."

These feeling are understandable and important. Nevertheless, not using a condom can have dangerous results. Although health professionals say that women are more likely to become HIV-infected from men, men can be infected by women.

Basketball superstar Earvin "Magic" Johnson contracted HIV through unprotected sex with a woman. So did professional heavyweight boxer Tommy Morrison.

Women often feel pressure from their partners not to use a condom. Young women sometimes feel that agreeing to have sex without a condom is a small thing to do in return for someone's love. However, you can't lose sight of your own needs, especially the need to protect yourself.

It is often difficult to be assertive. But women and men can learn "condom negotiation" techniques. These are techniques that allow you and your partner to discuss the use of condoms during sex. Each person discusses his or her concerns and desires and together the man and the woman can agree to use the condom. If one of the partners still refuses to wear a condom, then you should be thinking twice about having sex with him or her.

There's a larger picture here: understanding what it means to be an adult. A lot of being an adult

Fresh air and physical activity can contribute to your well-being.

is learning to live with limits. You can still enjoy yourself and express yourself in both sexual and nonsexual ways. You can hug or touch someone, expressing affection as well as sexual feelings. You can go out with your friends, go to concerts, do the things you like to do. You just have to do it with a view toward taking care of your health.   And you can take satisfaction in knowing that you are not putting anyone else at risk of HIV, and you are keeping yourself from being reinfected.

Having a Family

Young people who are HIV-positive face difficult decisions about whether or not to have a family. Some want this very badly. Yet babies born to HIV-positive mothers have about a 25 to 30 percent chance of remaining HIV-positive themselves.

Some health-care professionals who treat HIV-positive babies feel strongly that people with HIV should not risk having children. Others say that no one has the right to interfere with decisions about pregnancy and childbearing. Still others point out that HIV-positive children can live a long time, and that their lives should not be seen as less worth living just because they have HIV. Still another viewpoint says that people should not plan to have children if they are not sure they will be around to take care of them. All these different points of view can be debated. In the meantime, consult someone who will give you the facts and let you decide.

And what should *you* do? For some people, having a baby feels like a chance to leave something of value in the world. For some who decide to have a child, the odds that it will be healthy don't look so bad.

Claudia was pregnant with her second child when she found out she was HIV-positive. The way she found out was that her first child, a boy, had AIDS. He later died, so she knew firsthand the grief that comes with having an HIV-positive child. Now she was faced with a very difficult decision: "Do I want to have another child, knowing what I know and how it feels?" In the end, she decided to go ahead. "If I have an abortion, the baby will definitely die. At least now it has a chance. Maybe this one will live."

For others, the possibility of bearing a child who might develop AIDS is far too big a risk: they fear watching a child become progressively ill, or not being around to care for the child.

Marisa would not consider having another child for these reasons. She is very grateful that she had her daughter before contracting HIV. She knows her daughter will suffer a lot if she dies. She would not want to repeat this by having another child, whether or not that child turned out to be infected. In the same way, Steven wants children very much. Yet he feels that it's too much to ask someone to care for his children if he is not around to bring them up.

Pursuing the goals you have set for yourself is still very important.
Planning ahead will help you structure your life.

There is no right answer to these questions. Making the decision whether or not to have a child takes deep thought and discussion with your partner and people you trust.

Also remember that if you are HIV-positive and want to have a child, you must have unprotected sex. So this decision involves the health and well-being of three people: you, your partner, and a child-to-be.

If You Have Kids...

This is another area most kids your age don't have to think about as much as you do. It involves setting goals for yourself and your family, which was discussed in Chapter 6.

If you already have children, planning also involves thinking about their future. Where will they live? Who will take care of them?

Someone else taking care of your kids is called *custody* or *guardianship*. These terms have legal meanings and involve different ways of assuming responsibility. It's best to get help both from your family and from a caring professional, because these issues can be complicated.

Some young people with children have said that, although this issue was very difficult to face, they felt great relief in knowing that their children's futures were settled. They were able to have some control over how their children would be cared for, and this set their minds at rest.

Chapter 8

Keep Hope Alive!

Where there's life there's hope. A person infected with HIV sometimes finds that hard to believe. But the teens who told their stories at the beginning of this book have learned with time to have hope.

Evelyn, for instance, says, "It turned out that I do have HIV. My parents are hopeful that everything will turn out okay. On my bad days, I don't believe that's true. But on my good days, which happen more often than bad days, I think, hey, maybe they're right. I think I'll stick around to find out."

"I'm talking to support groups and individuals with HIV about how much better I've been feeling now that I'm taking protease inhibitors," Greg says. "Telling people that they may start feeling better is a hard sell, but as more people try these new therapies, the more they believe me."

Listen to the hope offered by Evelyn and Greg. Listen to the hope expressed by the people who care about you. And, most of all, listen to that small voice that tells you what you already know: Where there's life there's hope.

Glossary—*Explaining New Words*

AIDS Acquired immunodeficiency syndrome, the series of illnesses that infect a person whose immune system has been damaged by HIV.

anal sex Sexual act in which the penis is inserted in the partner's anus.

anonymous testing HIV testing in which no names are used, and no HIV status is written down anywhere.

AZT Drug often used to slow the effects of HIV.

condom Covering for the penis, which should be made of latex to protect against HIV.

confidential testing Testing for HIV done in a clinic or private office, where health-care workers are aware of your HIV status.

hemophilia Disease in which the blood does not clot properly. People with this disease need to inject blood products.

HIV Human immunodeficiency virus, the virus that causes AIDS.

informed consent Knowing what it means to be tested for HIV or to have medical treatment, and agreeing to it.

injecting drug use Using drugs that are injected into the body.

nonoxynol-9 Chemical in spermicides that is thought to kill HIV.

opportunistic infection An infection that takes
   advantage of a weakened immune system.
oral sex Sex act involving one person's mouth on
   another person's genitals.
retroviral drug Drug such as AZT used to slow the
   growth of HIV.
safer sex Sex using a latex condom.
sexually transmitted diseases (STDs) Diseases
   such as syphilis, gonorrhea, and chlamydia that are
   passed through sexual intercourse.
virus Small living organism that can grow and
   increase in the body and cause infection.

Where to Go for Help

The Adolescent AIDS Program
Montefiore Medical Center
111 East 210th Street
Bronx, NY 10467
(718) 882-0232

**The AIDS and Adolescent Network of
   New York, Inc.**
666 Broadway, Suite 520
New York, NY 10012
(212) 505-9115

Hot Lines
- AIDS Hot Line for Teens: (800) 234-TEEN
- Experiemental AIDS Therapies Hot Line: (800) 874-2572
- National AIDS Hot Line: (800) 342-AIDS
- National AIDS Hot Line (Spanish): (800) 344-SIDA
- National AIDS Hot Line TTY/TTD Service: (800) AIDS-TTY

You can call these numbers for AIDS-related questions and to get the number of the AIDS Hot line in your state. Remember, all 800 numbers are free.

- Pediatric and Pregnancy AIDS Hot line: (212) 227-8922

Information/Referral Numbers
- Black Americans and AIDS Project of the National Urban League: (212) 674-3500
- Hetrick Martin Institute for Gay and Lesbian Youth: (212) 633-8902
- Hispanic AIDS Forum: (212) 966-6336
- National AIDS Information Clearinghouse: (800) 458-5231
- National Network of Runaway and Youth Services: (202) 682-4114

For Further Reading

Blake, Jeanne. *Risky Times: How to Be AIDS-Smart and Stay Healthy*. New York: Workman Publishing, 1990.

Hein, Karen; Theresa Foy DiGeronimo; and the Editors of *Consumer Reports. AIDS: Trading Fears for Facts*. Yonkers, NY: Consumer Reports Books, 1991.

Kittredge, Mary. *Teens with AIDS Speak Out*. Thorndike, Maine: Thorndike Press, 1993

Mozen, Paula, producer. *No Rewind: Teenagers Speak Out on HIV/AIDS Awareness* (videorecording). San Francisco: CrossCurrent Media/NAATA, 1992.

Rubenstein, William, B. *The Rights of People Who Are HIV-Positive*. Carbondale, IL: Southern Illinois Press, 1996.

Swisher, Karin L., editor. *Teenage Sexuality: Opposing Viewpoints*. San Diego, CA: Greenhaven Press, 1994.

Wickwire, Peggy A. "Nutrition and HIV: Your Choices Make a Difference." Tennesee Department of Health and Environment, East Central AIDS Education and Training Center, Tennesee Office.

Index

A

AIDS
  difference between HIV and, 12
  Hot line, 29
  symptoms of, 13
anger, 24, 25, 46
antiviral drugs, 40–41

B

blood products, 14–15

C

clinical trials, 42
Commission on Human Rights, 35
condom, 18–19, 51–52
confidentiality, 29–30
consent (for testing), 33–34
coping (with HIV), 47
counseling, 46

D

denial, 21–22
Department of Public Health, 29
disclosure, 49–50

E

ELISA test, 11
exercise, 43–44

F

fear, 21, 22, 46

H

having a family (with HIV), 54–55, 57
hemophilia, 8, 25
HIV
  medicines for, 40
  prevention of, 15–16
  testing for, 29–30, 33
  transmission of, 14–15
  virus that causes, 11
homosexuality, 27, 38
hugging, 15

I

immune system, 10, 12, 13, 15, 39

J

Johnson, Magic, 52

About the Author
Amy Shire has a master's degree in Public Health from Columbia University and is a program planner with the New York City Division of AIDS Services. She also teaches a course in AIDS and public policy at the New York University School of Continuing Education Adult Degree Program.

Photo Credits
Cover photo by Dick Smolinski; pp. 2, 32 © AP/Wide World Photos; pp. 6, 23 by Chris Volpe; pp. 14, 17, 20, 36, 41, 45, 48, 53, 56 by Stuart Rabinowitz; pp. 26, 31 by Mary Lauzon.